Hotels for the Hopeful

*Land promoters promise a perfect life
of health, wealth, and pleasure
in Monte Vista.*

**The Early History of Sunland, California
Volume 1**

ML Tiernan

Hotels for the Hopeful

www.maryleetiernan.com
Second printing April 1, 2015
10 9 8 7 6 5 4 3 2

ISBN 978-0983067207 (Paperback)

©1999 ©2010 Mary Lee Tiernan. All rights reserved. No portion of this product may be photographed, scanned, translated, reproduced, copied, or reduced to any tangible or electronic medium or machine-readable form, without the prior written consent of Mary Lee Tiernan.

Photograph on cover courtesy of Bolton Hall Museum, Tujunga, California.
Quote on cover from advertisements for Monte Vista.

Contents

The Land Boom of the 1880s 5

Simple Beginnings 9

Homestyle Hospitality 15

The Grand and Elegant 21

Original Maps for the Village of Monte Vista 31

Footnotes 33

Bibliography 35

The Early History of Sunland, California series 40

Author's Notes

The researcher, like a detective, examines the evidence to try to determine the real story. Unfortunately for researchers, we cannot re-examine witnesses or revisit scenes because in most cases, they have long since disappeared. So we sort through the conflicting data to find the most reliable and logical explanations. I have done my best to follow the clues and weave as authentic a story as possible.

My thanks to the staff at Bolton Hall Museum, Tujunga, California, for their assistance with this project.

The Land Boom of the 1880s

When the Southern Pacific Railroad finished the line connecting Los Angeles to San Francisco in 1876, it completed the last leg of the transcontinental railroad. The timing was perfect. After the Civil War, people began migrating westward. The real estate boom in the Midwest had just about run its course when the Southern Pacific provided access to even more new territory by opening Southern California for settlement. Spying the opportunity for new fortunes, speculators rushed to California. "They came here not to build up the country, but to make money, honestly, if they could not make it any other way."[1]

These veteran promoters would create the impression of a town-in-progress by building a hotel and laying sidewalks or curbs. Often they began construction on bogus railroad stations because a railroad line through town promised future prosperity. Smooth-talking, confident, and unrestrained by honesty, they sold lots in towns built of air. Between 1884 and 1886, speculators platted 100 towns in Los Angeles County; 62 of them no longer exist.

Because the railroad companies needed to recoup the fortune spent in building lines across the desert, and because they wanted to ensure future business and profit, they eagerly encouraged the westward migration. They hired agents who hawked the glories of California across the United States and Europe. Special emigrant cars carried hopefuls to the 'promised land.' Because trains dropped the dining cars once they passed the Mississippi River, passengers brought bread and food in tins with them. A stove in the rear of the car allowed travelers to heat water or make coffee. For sleeping, the seats folded out into beds. To alleviate the harshness of travel, the train stopped during the day to allow passengers to exercise. Some trains carried entertainers or a clergyman for Sunday services. The railroad also furnished excursion trains for larger groups seeking to settle a colony.

But the opening of a second line, the Santa Fe, in 1886, broke the Southern Pacific's monopoly and sparked an explosion unparalleled elsewhere. Competition for passengers ignited a price war between the two companies. The usual rate of $125 for fare from Missouri to California began to drop. As one company decreased its price, the other undercut it. Prices fell drastically. On March 6, 1887, the Santa Fe actually reduced the fare to $1 per passenger.

Low rates inspired even more settlers, tourists, and sightseers to embark toward the Pacific shores and

California's glorious climate. After completion of the Southern Pacific, the population increased 100 times. After the Santa Fe line opened, the population multiplied 500 times. California exploded from 5,000 to 100,000 in only 20 years.

The avalanche of visitors accorded speculators golden opportunities for fleecing the public. Copywriters used alluring language, made wild promises, and even lied. In this war to attract prospective buyers, claims were as outlandish as the imagination allowed. One promoter went as far as sticking oranges on Joshua trees in the desert and

Sunland 1909 looking toward the entrance to Big Tujunga Canyon.
Photo courtesy of Bolton Hall Museum.

claimed they grew there naturally.

The ads for Monte Vista followed this same pattern. In one ad, the promoters promised, "Four miles only from the S.P.R.R. (Southern Pacific Railroad) and four railroads looking towards it with the certainty of one being built within a year, and no possibility of passing around it."[2] Of course, the railroad never materialized. One unusual difference in the promoters' approach was the construction of a working water system before plots were offered for sale. But ads exaggerated the abundance of water, the richness of the soil, and most of all, the climate, one of the prime attractions to California. Although the clean, clear air in Monte Vista really was good, who would believe that "The very instant the invalid reaches Monte Vista, improvement begins and continues until perfect health and strength are recovered. Who will not gain health here is beyond hope."[3]

But for all their efforts, they failed. When the land boom died at the end of the 1880s and the dust settled, Monte Vista was considered one of the towns that didn't make it. The farmers and entrepreneurs persevered, however, and eventually the village called Sunland thrived.

Simple Beginnings

When travelers descended from the train at Roscoe depot, they could walk the four and a half miles up Roscoe Blvd. to Monte Vista or take the 'stage.' Most, of course, chose the stage. Unlike the more elaborate version pictured in Western films, a simple horse and buggy escorted passengers over the rough roads. Even when a pickup truck, with wood benches running along the sides of the bed, later replaced the horse and buggy, one still referred

John Johnson (center) greeted visitors at his Monte Vista Inn after their dusty ride to the village. Photo Courtesy of Bolton Hall Museum.

to it as the 'stagecoach.'

As the stagecoach ascended the last knoll, Watson Hill, and cruised to the level land around the park, it stopped at John J. Johnson's Monte Vista Inn. In the early 1880s, Johnson converted a small hunting lodge into a public inn to greet visitors after the bumpy, difficult ride to the village.

In warm weather, John stood behind a counter under the shade of a large pine serving bottled drinks and snacks. Of course, ice wasn't available, but the drinks still refreshed thirsty throats after that dusty ride on dirt roads. Wooden benches around the base of the tree provided seating for his customers. The outside 'bar' stretched between the inn and his house.

John J. Johnson
Photo from Bolton Hall Museum

The inn's founder was the son of Farmer A. Johnson, one of the original homesteaders in the Monte Vista Valley. Like his father and brothers, John[4] homesteaded land in Big Tujunga Canyon, where he hived bees. But unlike his father and brothers who lived in the more remote canyon, John preferred living and working in the center of town. Official records from 1911 show John paid a total of $4.11 in taxes on his two parcels of choice land across from Sunland Park.

Living in town allowed John to take advantage of improvements as the village grew. The telephone arrived in 1908, when 22 subscribers invested $2,200 to found the Sunland Rural Telephone Company. In the beginning, service was limited to one and a half hours each morning and evening. A single line ran up the valley from Glendale to the switchboard, housed in the home of the operator. With only one line, the whole village could tune in at the same time. Not much chance of privacy in those early days! But as the company grew, John and the other

The inn became a popular dance pavilion named Twin Pines in the 1920s.
Photo from The Record-Ledger, June 18, 1964.

shareholders would reap sizable financial rewards.

The inn served other purposes over the years as a post office, a confectionary store, an open-air theater, and a dance pavilion. When the outdoor pavilion opened in September 1923, the name of the inn changed to Twin Pines, a fitting tribute to the large trees growing on either side of the entrance. As the price of admission opening night, attendees donated a quart of fruit or jam to the home for underprivileged children then operating at the Monte Vista Hotel. Dancing continued at the inn, or Twin Pines, until 1931.

When John died two years later in 1933, his property

Bulldozers crushed the old inn just short of its 100th birthday.
The name was still visible on the worn wood.
Photo from of The Record-Ledger, June 18, 1964.

passed on to his heirs. Eventually, they sold the property and the inn was condemned.

Bulldozers crushed the dilapidated Monte Vista Inn close to its 100th birthday in 1964. By then, boards covered the windows and doors, and very few traces of paint remained on the worn wood walls. Only the large letters spelling out the name of the inn were still visible.

Sunland Park in the 1880-1890s. Photo courtesy of Bolton Hall Museum.

The Park Hotel welcomed early visitors to Sunland.
Photo from The Record-Ledger, August 8, 1968.

Homestyle Hospitality

Anna Jump liked to sit in her rocking chair on the porch, a popular activity in times past, and watch life in town pass by. Her husband Sid preferred a more active routine, watering and pruning the gardens which surrounded the house. Inside, President Harding greeted visitors from the wall, pressed wood chairs awaited guests around the dining table, and a hand-wound Victrola played in the parlor. Basins and pitchers on the bureaus in the bedrooms offered the weary a chance to wash up before climbing into high iron beds to sleep. Such was the life in the Jump house in the 1960s!

The eight-room home, with four bedrooms upstairs and one bedroom and one bath downstairs, functioned as a hotel for almost 50 years. Sources conflict on the origin of the Park Hotel. Some sources credit Frank H. Barclay with building it as a home for his wife and three daughters, who lived there before the completion of his Monte Vista Hotel just down the street. Other sources credit Sherman Page and F.C. Howes, the original land speculators in the Monte Vista Valley, with its construction.

Page and Howes bought about 2,200 acres of the original Rancho Tujunga in 1883. That same year, they filed a claim for water rights to Big Tujunga Canyon and built a water system to divert water to their property. They platted 40 acres of the land for a town; the remaining acreage would be sold as farmland. In the center of the future town, a grove of majestic live oaks stretched their branches. They preserved an oval-shaped piece of the grove, bisecting Sherman and Central Avenues, for a park. On a site facing the oak grove park, they commissioned the building of a hotel where potential buyers could stay while inspecting the land. An ad in the *Rural Californian* dated

Rear view of the Park Hotel. Photo courtesy of Bolton Hall Museum.

November 1885 refers to that hotel when it promises that "All expenses incurred by purchase of land after leaving Los Angeles, including hack fare and hotel bills, will be deducted from the purchase price." Page and Howes named their village Monte Vista.

The only structure in early Monte Vista that could be Page and Howes' hotel is the Park Hotel. In addition, sources do agree that the building dates back to 1884 or 1885. It is more probable, therefore, that credit for its construction goes to Page and Howes. Barclay didn't buy the land from them until 1886[5] when construction on the Monte Vista Hotel began.

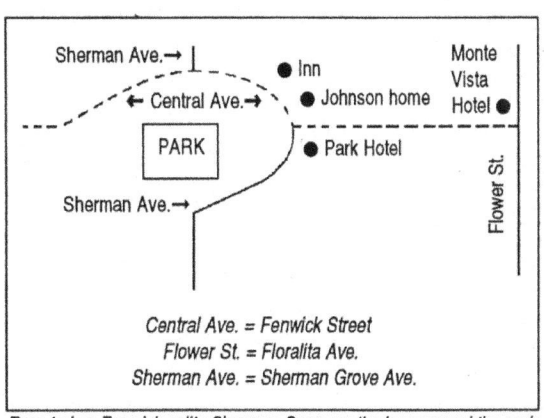

Even today, Fenwick splits Sherman Grove on the loop around the park.

The Park Hotel, on the corner of Central and Sherman Avenues, welcomed the earliest overnight visitors to Monte Vista. It faced the park from which it derived its name: originally referred to as Live Oak Park, the name changed to Monte Vista Park, then to Sunland Park. On the hotel's north side, just across the dirt road, stood the Monte Vista Inn.

After the Barclays moved out, Ben Willis and his wife, nicknamed Aunt Randy, managed the hotel. Publicity and news accounts often overlooked the smaller hotel, claiming the Monte Vista Hotel to be the first hotel, but not always. An advertisement for land sales in *The Los Angeles Times* from 1887 stresses accommodations in the larger and more luxurious Monte Vista Hotel, but mentions the "...Park Hotel, a smaller house, but equally neat and clean, but conducted on a lower scale of prices, faces the grand oak grove."[6] Rooms at the Park rented for $2.50 a night; those at the Monte Vista Hotel for $3 to $4 a night.

By 1906, Los Angeles had definitely established itself as a major Western city with all the conveniences a thriving metropolis can offer. Nevertheless, Anna Brandstetter and her husband sold their city home, packed up three-year-old Herbert, and headed for the largely unsettled Monte Vista Valley. Although considered a 'ghost town' by some historians because of its failure to establish itself during the boom of the 1880s, those who had moved to Monte Vista planted their feet as well as grapes and olives, peaches and apricots, oranges and lemons.

After buying the Park Hotel and a 13-acre farm, the Brandstetters adjusted to rustic life in the country. Only Rowley's General Store, and the butcher who came from San Fernando once a week to deliver fresh meat, offered the luxury of outside amenities. Just getting to the Roscoe train station often meant a four-and-a-half-mile walk.

While her husband tended the peach grove and vineyard, Anna cared for their home, their lodgers, and their son Herbert, one of only five children in the original Sunland school. Anna cooked and baked on a wood-burning stove, sewed her own clothes by the light of a kerosene lamp, and drew needed water from a well with a bucket. Their few hours of free time limited recreation to picnics in the park across the street. However grueling the life of those pioneer farmers, Anna later reminisced, "Perhaps I was foolish to leave my home in Los Angeles, but it was just what we wanted, and we were happy. I wish I had it back now."[7]

Several years later, the trees in their orchard stopped bearing fruit because of droughts and the increasing demand on the water supply from newcomers to the valley. The Brandstetters sold their farm acreage, but kept their home and continued welcoming guests. After Mr. Brandsetter died in 1924, Anna married Sidney (Sid) Jump. The doors to the Park Hotel stayed open into the 1930s when the Jumps retired. Townsfolk renamed the old

Park Hotel the Jump House because of Sid's familiar figure in the garden and Anna's on the porch, finally resting after her years of toil. Both died in 1965.

The 1971 earthquake shook the building until floors buckled, walls sloped at odd angles, and the porch jutted out over the front steps. The irreparable damage spelled death for the then-oldest structure in Sunland. A small apartment house replaced it.

Irreparable damage from the 1971 earthquake doomed the old house.
Photo from The Record-Ledger, February 14, 1971.

The Grand and Elegant

At the height of the land boom in 1887, $100 million worth of land sold in Los Angeles County alone. But by 1886, only a couple of dozen people had actually settled in Monte Vista, with about 250 acres of land under irrigation. Page and Howes were probably glad to unload their unsold land to Frank H. Barclay for a large profit. Unfortunately for Barclay, he bought toward the end of the boom.

Exaggerated advertising flourished during the 1880s as speculators competed with each other trying to attract buyers. Barclay's ads to entice visitors to Monte Vista followed that pattern. "…just right for the growing of all the finest California fruits … The air is absolutely pure and dry … delicate persons may hope for life, health and strength in the glorious climate of Monte Vista … (water) is absolutely pure and clear as crystal and practically unlimited."[8]

Barclay's imagination soared in his description of Monte Vista Park with "terraces planted in ornamental flowers and plants, while hammocks and swings, benches

The elegant Monte Vista Hotel, pictured here just after its construction, offered first class amenities to its guests.
Photo courtesy of Bolton Hall Museum.

and chairs make attractions that elsewhere cannot be had, while beautiful fountains make a delicious music for those who are ill or those who are well."[9] In reality, the park was then simply a grove of oak trees where Barclay and others enjoyed excellent rabbit hunting.

The small Park Hotel seemed inadequate for the crowds Barclay hoped to attract to Monte Vista. A larger, more elegant hotel could not only house potential buyers, but attract vacationers. So at the extravagant cost of $30,000[10] Barclay started construction of the Monte Vista

Hotel on the corner of Central Avenue (Fenwick Street) and Flower (Floralita) Avenue in 1886. When it opened in 1887, an advertisement described the Monte Vista Hotel as "...the most charming resort ... Absolutely first-class in every detail ... nothing is left undone to make it absolutely a model hotel."[11] This, at least, was true.

The luxurious Victorian offered comfort in elegantly furnished rooms; each room featured a fireplace for warmth, and ventilation for hot days. Amenities included gas lighting, a fire-alarm system, a large dining room with a pine dance floor, service with fine china and silver, and a unique two-story privy. The observatory on the tower offered a panoramic view of the valley, or guests could relax on the twelve-foot-wide veranda encircling the hotel.

As Barclay hoped, the hotel lured the wealthy who enjoyed 'the country' in elegant style. The amenities offered by the hotel, among them the fine cuisine by a French chef, outweighed the difficulties of traveling to the remote village. In the beginning, visitors took the train to Glendale and then transferred to the stage for the remainder of the trip to the hotel. Later, long after Barclay lost the hotel, they arrived in fashionable Model T's, to the delight of local children.

Whether because of the exaggerated advertising, the promises of free barbecues and beer busts, or the luxurious hotel, crowds of people flocked to the Monte Vista Hotel

THE MONTE VISTA HOTEL
A COUNTRY HOTEL BILL OF FARE

SOUP
Oyster   Vegetable

HORS D'OEUVRES
Sliced Cucumbers   Sliced Tomatoes

SMALL PATTIES
Fish   Baked Salmon   Potatoes Hollandaise

REMOVES
Roast Sirloin of Beef, Brown Gravy

Roast Spring Chicken, Fresh Green Peas

Roast Saddle of Veal with Dressing

SALAD
Lettuce   Lobster

Potato   Shrimp

ENTREES
Stewed Eggs, Alsatian Sauce   Mushrooms

French Pancake with Jelly   Asparagus on Toast

VEGETABLES
Mashed Irish Potatoes   Boiled Sweet Potatoes

Summer Squash   Fresh Green Peas

Stewed Tomatoes

DESSERT
Stewed Fruit Pudding, Brandy Sauce

Lemon Pie   Apple Pie   Raspberry Pie

Vanilla Ice Cream   Lemon Ice Cream

Assorted Cookies

Fruit   Crackers   Cheese

on weekends. From the observatory tower on the third floor of the hotel, Barclay showed perspective buyers a bird's-eye view of the land and pointed out general locations of plots for sale. Many bought un-surveyed and un-staked plots from that tower without taking the time to check specific locations. Barclay simply marked the sales on a map. Unfortunately for the buyers, Barclay failed to officially record the map or the deeds he gave to them, and lawsuits resulted for the next 20 years. Other settlers often quitclaimed[12] the land that buyers could not identify.

Barclay himself lived at the hotel with his wife and three daughters: Anna, Edith, and Mary. Anna earned a reputation in the village as an energetic tomboy. She married and remained in the area as Mrs. Kirby, known for her interest in studying foreign languages.

Mary met a tragic fate at age 20. After sharing an evening with friends in Burbank, she started home about 5:00 a.m. the next morning, dropped off a friend, and continued the journey alone in her horse-drawn carriage. At 8:20, midway between Roscoe and Monte Vista, a mail carrier found her body with her head wedged between a shaft and wheel of the carriage. Miss Phillips extricated the body, put the dead woman in the carriage, and brought Mary on her last journey home. The coroner's inquest ruled that Mary had apparently suffered from one of her epileptic seizures on the way home and had fallen head-

A side view of the Monte Vista taken years later shows the hotel had lost its tower, but trees and vines softened the landscape.
Photo courtesy of Bolton Hall Museum.

first between the shaft and the wheel. Unwittingly, the horse continued a few paces, fracturing her skull and "crushing her life out"[13] with a few revolutions of the wheel. Without a guiding hand, the horse finally stopped and waited patiently until Phillips found them.

What happened to other members of the family is unknown.

Barclay went bankrupt in 1888 with the demise of the land boom and lost the hotel. Dr. Quintin Rowley, brother of town leader Loron Rowley, bought it as an investment. The elegant hotel enjoyed years of popularity with sportsmen hunting in nearby canyons, with families vacationing in clean country air, and as a retreat for Los

Angles businessmen. It even had its scandals. "In 1908 a district attorney from Los Angles got caught with a woman at that hotel and it caused quite a ruckus," recalled an original settler, Paul Lancaster.[14]

The luxurious resort began its swan song during the First World War. In 1920 the Council of Community Service of the State of California bought the hotel to convert it to a home for undernourished children in Los Angeles County. The announcement in the *Glendale Evening News*, December 20, 1920, ran with emotional appeal for "future citizens of the republic, (who) will be fostered and cherished and brought to the full physical development that is their birthright." Community leaders John Steven McGroarty and M.V. Hartranft agreed to pay

The removal of the third story, the mansard roof, and the gingerbread woodwork ruined any historical value of the old hotel.
Photo courtesy of Bolton Hall Museum.

$500 for necessary repair work. "All the Boy Scouts of the county will be privileged to take charge of the clearing up and beautifying of the grounds."

The hotel as Cyprus Manor. Trees and weeds grew taller as the stature of the hotel dwindled. Photo courtesy of Bolton Hall Museum.

Mrs. R.W. Meeker of Glendale chaired efforts to furnish the kitchen, asking clubs and organizations to "…give just one good, aluminum utensil … for anything that benefits future citizens of our country should concern every patriotic citizen of the land, and claim his aid as far as he is able to give it." Despite all the emotional appeal, the home was not a success and closed its doors.

In 1923, the Volunteers of America refurbished the inside of the building as a home for the elderly and replaced the original wood foundation with stone. The next year, they 'modified' the outside by tearing down the top story, building a veranda around the second story, adding French doors from the rooms onto the veranda, and refinishing the outside walls with stucco.

The remodeling, especially the removal of the third story, the mansard roof, and the gingerbread woodwork, eliminated the features typical of Victorian architecture. Although the old hotel would continue to function as a rest home for many years, the "green monstrosity … (now had) very little worth saving from an historical standpoint."[15]

The history of the last years of the hotel is sketchy. In 1948, the Volunteers of America celebrated the 25th anniversary of their rest home. In 1950, Harry Morrill, a

When the bulldozers arrived, only vandals and children stepped through the doorways of the 'haunted house.'
Photo from The Record-Ledger, April 9, 1964.

local builder, bought the home with the intention of making it a 'club house' for civic and service organizations with meeting rooms, a banquet hall, and recreational facilities. This apparently did not happen. In 1954, Mr. and Mrs. Robert Christopher bought the building, repainted and repaired it, and opened the Cypress Manor rest home, which closed in 1959.

Ruin replaced Victorian splendor. Vandals visited the once grand hotel, smashing windows, writing on walls, and strewing broken bottles across the floors. Neighbors, fearful for the safety of children investigating the 'haunted house,' petitioned for its destruction. In 1964 demolition crews moved in. "…the old building, constructed of grade A lumber, all center cut and without a single knot hole, stayed erect as long as possible against the bulldozer's relentless onslaughts."[16] Eventually, of course, the bulldozer won, crushing it and several other neighboring structures between Sherman Grove and Floralita. In the cleared area rose houses and apartment buildings.

#####

Original Maps for Monte Vista

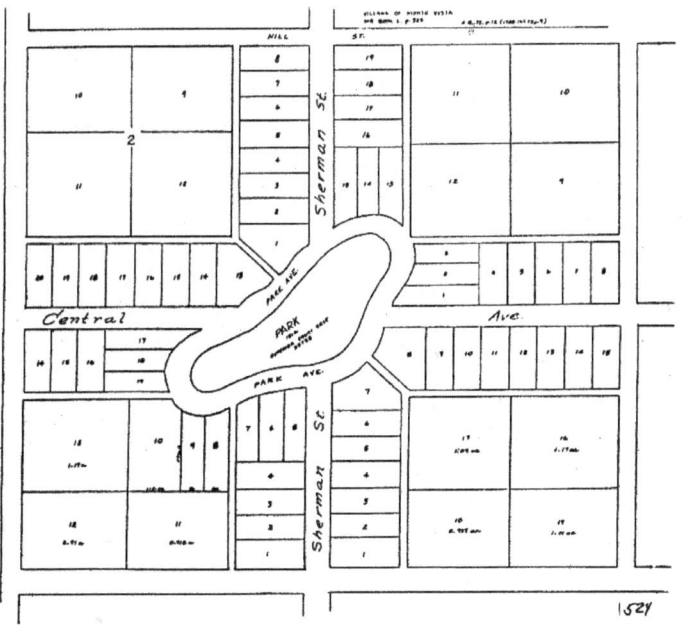

Plat Map 1

This plat map is thought to be the first design of the village by the original promoters, Sherman Page and F.C. Howes.

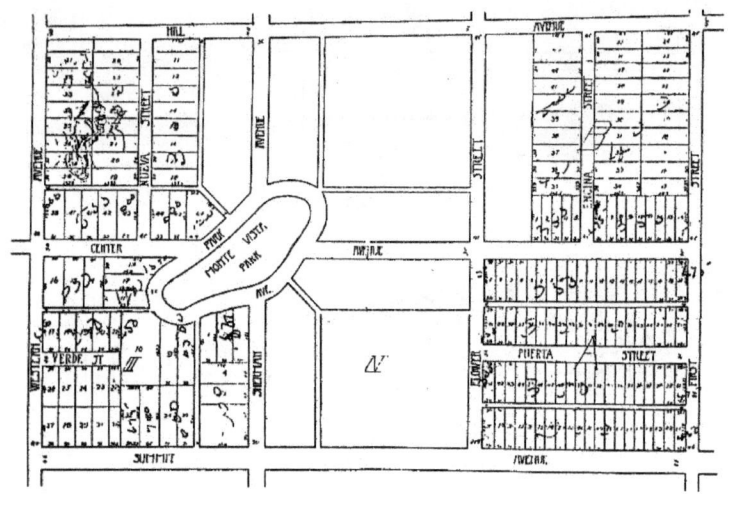

Plat Map 2

This revised plat map was mostly likely Frank Barclay's plan, after he bought the land from Page and Howes. Prices ranged from $300 to $650 per lot. Note that some sections are not divided into lots, indicating the land was not for sale.

Footnotes

[1] Cleland, Robert Glass, *From Wilderness to Empire: A History of California 1542-1900*. New York: Alfred A. Knopf, 1944, p. 357.

[2] Advertisement, *Los Angeles Daily Herald*, June 6, 1887.

[3] Advertisement, *Los Angeles Times*, Friday, July 1, 1887.

[4] John Joseph Johnson: born November 4, 1862 – died February 7, 1933.

[5] A legal document that belonged to Frank Barclay mentions the date June 19, 1886, as the date of "… the Abstract … relating to that portion of the Rancho Tujunga conveyed by F.C. Howes and Sherman Page to F.H. Barclay, et al. by deed …"

[6] Advertisement, *Los Angeles Times*, Friday, July 1, 1887.

[7] "Six Persons Owned Valley When Anna Jump Arrived," *The Record-Ledger*, Thursday, September 30, 1954, A-4.

[8] Advertisement, *Los Angeles Times*, Friday, July 1, 1887.

[9] Ibid.

[10] Some sources claim the hotel cost $20,000 to build; others claim $30,000.

[11] Advertisement, *Los Angeles Times*, Friday, July 1, 1887.

[12] Quitclaim: to release a legal claim, especially on a parcel of real estate, without a warranty of title. In this case, since owners could not identify their parcels of land, others who settled on the land claimed it since the owners "quit" it.

[13] "Killed on the Road," Clippings file, Bolton Hall Museum.

[14] "He Was Here in the Beginning," *The Record-Ledger*, February 12, 1986.

[15] "Cypress Manor Passes into Oblivion," *The Record-Ledger*, April 9, 1964.

[16] <u>Ibid</u>.

Bibliography

Advertisement. *Los Angeles Daily Herald*, June 6, 1887.

Advertisement. *Los Angeles Times*, Friday, July 1, 1887.

Advertisement. *Los Angeles Times*, Sunday, July 3, 1887.

Advertisement. November 1885. Clippings file, Bolton Hall Museum.

Advertisement. *Rural Californian*, November 1884.

Advertisement. *Rural Californian*, November 1885.

"Advertisement in LA Times Dated 1887 Boasts Marvels of Monte Vista: Los Angeles Times, Friday, July 1, 1887." *The Record-Ledger*, September 27, 1973.

"Anna Kirby's Father Built Community's First Hotel." *The Record-Ledger*, September 30, 1954.

Austin, Lee. "Hostelry Built in 1887 Soon to Be Demolished." *Los Angeles Times*, Sunday, January 12, 1964.

Barclay, Frank H. Copies of personal papers and legal documents.

Boales, Jane. "Recalling Old Monte Vista Hotels." *The Record-Ledger*, October 20, 1979.

"Born at Old Monte Vista Hotel Speaker Revives Past of Area." *The Record-Ledger*, Thursday, February 11, 1974, p. 11.

Carlson, Viola. "Monte Vista Park Hotel: Oldest Building in Sunland-Tujunga." 1968.

Cleland, Robert Glass. *The Cattle on a Thousand Hills: Southern California, 1850-1880.* San Marino, CA: The Huntington Library. 1951.

Cleland, Robert Glass. *From Wilderness to Empire: A History of California, 1542-1900.* New York: Alfred A. Knopf. 1944.

"Cypress Manor Passes into Oblivion." *The Record-Ledger*, April 9, 1964.

Dumpke, Glenn S. *The Boom of the Eighties in Southern California.* San Marino, CA: Huntington Library. 1991.

Egremont, Angela. "Monte Vista Hotel: Important to Sunland-Tujunga Past." *The Leader*, Wednesday, August 30, 1989. p. 5."1880s – Boom and Bust Days in Southland." *Daily News*, date unknown.

Green Verdugo Hills: A Chronicle of Sunland-Tujunga, Calif. and How It Grew. Tujunga, CA: The Record-Ledger of the Verdugo Hills.

Harn, Jay. "He Was Here in the Beginning." *The Record-Ledger*, February 12, 1986.

Hartranft, M.V. "Monte Vista Park." *The Western Empire Land-Banking and Home Securing Plan*. January, 1911.

"Historic Hotel May Become Hub of Civic Life." *Glendale NewsPress*, Wednesday, April 19, 1950.

Hitt, Marlene. "Everyone Invited to Visit the Monte Vista Park Hotel." *Foothill Leader*, June 13, 1998.

"Hunting Lodge for Wealthy of 1870s on Skids." (sic) *Los Angeles Times*, September 10, 1961.

"Killed on the Road." Clippings file, Bolton Hall Museum.

"Landmark Ruined." *The Record-Ledger*, Sunday, February 14, 1971.

Little Landers Historical Society. *Docent Handbook*. Bolton Hall Museum.

"Los Angeles and the Land Boom of the 1880s." *Network: Los Angeles Network for Education in Local and California History*. June 1984. Vol. 3, No. 4.

McWilliams, Carey. *Southern California: An Island on the Land.* Salt Lake City: Peregrine Smith Books. 1973.

Miller, Charles. "Sunland-Tujunga's Ties to Hollywood." *Foothill Leader*, September 7, 1988.

"Monte Vista Hotel: Important to Sunland-Tujunga's Past." *The Leader*, Wednesday, August 30, 1989. p. 5.

"Monte Vista Hotel 1887 Country Hotel Bill of Fare." Bolton Hall Museum.

"Old Building to Look Like New." *The Record-Ledger*, October 16, 1924.

"Old Jump Home Open to Tours During S-T Old Timers Week." *The Record-Ledger*, August 8, 1968.

Page, Sherman. "Monte Vista." Henry E. Huntington Library, Pasadena, California.

Plat maps of Monte Vista. Bolton Hall Museum.

"Refitting Monte Vista Lodge for New Purpose." *The Record-Ledger*, November 22, 1923.

"Rowley Recalls Early Days of Sunland-Tujunga." *The Record-Ledger*, Thursday, September 27, 1973.

Rowley, Robert. Personal interview by Viola Carlson. 1974.

"Saga of Monte Vista." *The Record-Ledger*, Thursday, June 18, 1964.

"Six Persons Owned Valley When Anna Jump Arrived." *The Record-Ledger*, Thursday, September 30, 1954. A-4.

"Son of Late William C. Graham Recalls Coming to Sunland in 1909 with Father." *The Record-Ledger*, September 30, 1954. A-3.

"Starting Semi-Weekly Dances at Monte Vista Inn." *The Record-Ledger*, May 24, 1923.

"Story of One Little Wire and How It Grew." *The Record-Ledger*, Historical & Progress Edition, May 21, 1953.

"Sunland First Developed in Big 1887 Land Boom." *The Record-Ledger*, September 12, 1968.

Sunland-Tujunga: Nestled between the Verdugo Hills and the San Gabriel Mts. The Sunland-Tujunga Chamber of Commerce. March 1947.

"Telephone Company Office." *The Record-Ledger*, Thursday, July 28, 1955.

"This Is the Hotel that Was." *The Record-Ledger*, April 8, 1964.

"To Open Home for Aged at Sunland." *The Record-Ledger*, Thursday, December 13, 1923.

"Tujunga, 'Home of Health' Has Many Sanitariums, Rest Homes for Aged." *The Record-Ledger*, Thursday, August 16, 1956.

"Volunteers of America, Sunland Guest Home to Have Children." *The Record-Ledger*, Thursday, August 19, 1948.

The Early History of Sunland, California

8 Volume Series
Also available as ebooks

Vol. 1 *Hotels for the Hopeful* Land promoters of the 1880s promised a perfect life of health, wealth, and pleasure. Although their promises fell short of reality, the village did grow and prosper in the hands of farmers.

Vol. 2 *The Roscoe Robbers and the Sensational Train Robbery of 1894* Two robbers posed as passengers to flag down the train. When the engineer recognized danger, he opened the throttle and sped past. The bandits threw the spur switch, and the train careened full speed off the tracks.

Vol. 3 *The Parson and His Cemetery* Parson Wornum was so loved that when he died, the whole village attended his funeral. Years of neglect of his cemetery spelled disaster in 1978 when heavy rains tore open graves and washed bodies down the hillside.

Vol. 4 *From Crackers to Coal Oil* When a student pulled out his gun and laid it on his desk, the tiny one-room school found itself needing a new teacher. That brought Virginia Newcomb, a romance, and a new family that helped to develop the town, leaving behind a detailed account of pioneer life in a small village.

Vol. 5 *He Never Came Home* Joe Ardizzone, a local grape-grower, doubled as a hit-man for the Mafia. During Prohibition, Joe's bootlegging activities caught him in the middle of in-house quarreling. In 1931, he left on a short trip and disappeared into the pages of history.

Vol. 6 *Lancasters Lake* When Edgar Lancaster dredged the swamp on his land, he created a lake which became a treasured landmark. For 25 years, visitors flocked to its cool shores, and Hollywood used the lake as a set location for some of its early movies.

Vol. 7 *Living in Big Tujunga Canyon* Early settlers, like the Johnson family, found their way into the canyon, a dense woodland bristling with wildlife. 50 years later, the Webber family faced the wrath of the river now winding down a denuded mountainside.

Vol. 8 *From Whence They Came* The Land Boom of the 1880s brought immigrants from around the world. Two generations of Blumfields survived the difficulties of farming and water shortages through industry and imagination.

www.ingramcontent.com/pod-product-compliance
Lightning Source LLC
Chambersburg PA
CBHW061347040426
42444CB00011B/3127